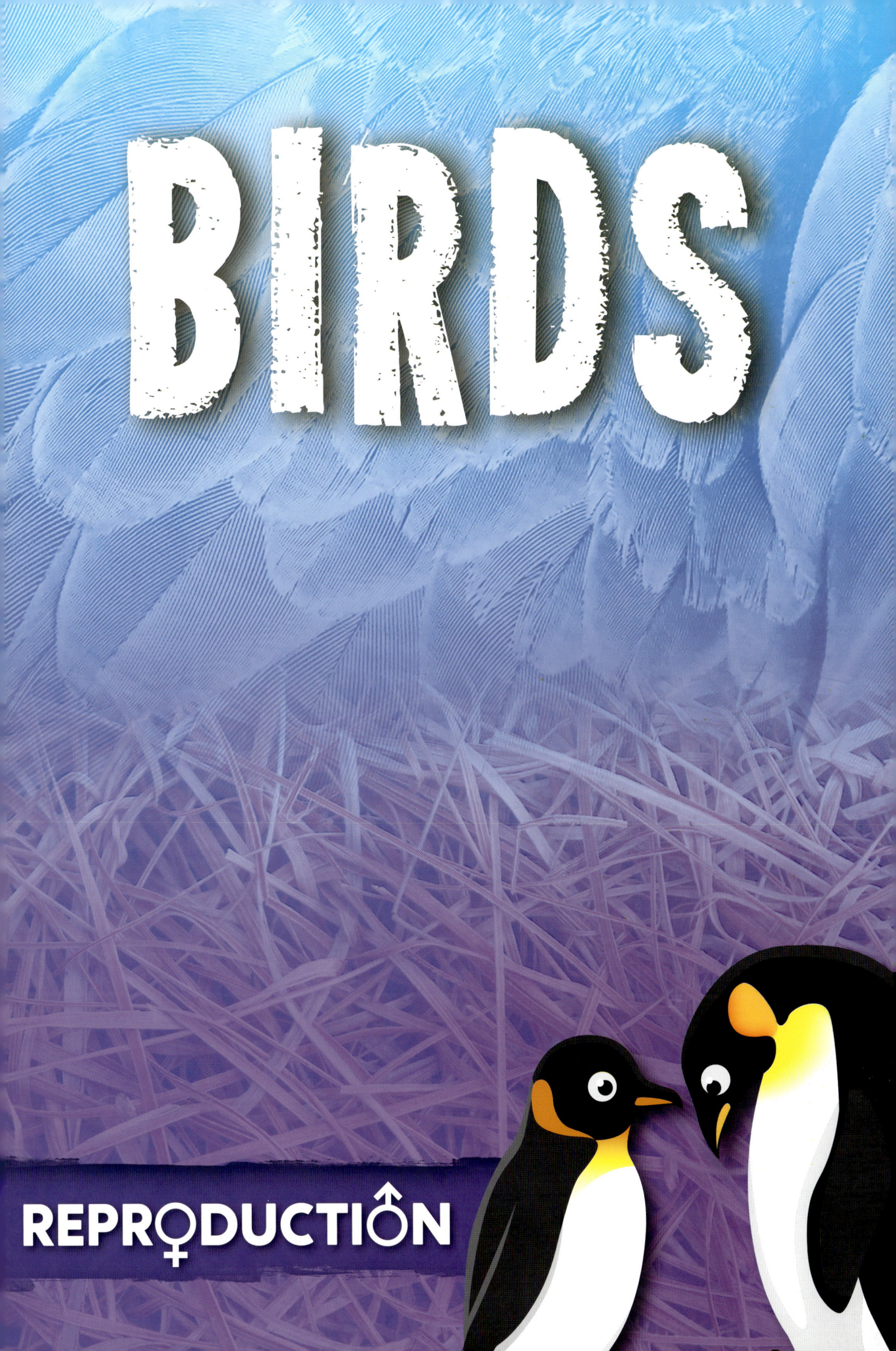

# BookLife
## PUBLISHING

©2019
BookLife Publishing Ltd.
King's Lynn
Norfolk PE30 4LS

All rights reserved.
Printed in Malaysia.

A catalogue record for this book is available from the British Library.

ISBN: 978-1-78637-674-9

Written by:
Joanna Brundle

Edited by:
John Wood

Designed by:
Ian McMullen

All facts, statistics, web addresses and URLs in this book were verified as valid and accurate at time of writing. No responsibility for any changes to external websites or references can be accepted by either the author or publisher.

## PHOTO CREDITS

All images are courtesy of Shutterstock.com, unless otherwise specified. With thanks to Getty Images, Thinkstock Photo and iStockphoto. Front Cover – sirtravelalot. 2 sirtravelalot. 4 – Monkey Business Images, Super Prin. 5 – BlueRingMedia, Christina Siow. 6 – Vladimir. Plish, paula french. 7 – Natalia Kuzmina, Karin Jaehne. 8 – Frank Wasserfuehrer, Ondrej Prosicky. 9 – Vishnevskiy Vasily, Sean McConnery. 10 – Peteri, Worakit Sirijinda. 11 – Olexandr Panchenko, Risto Puranen. 12 – Andrew Linscott, Heather L. Hubbard. 13 – finchfocus, TashaBubo, Mauricio S Ferreira. 14 – trabantos, David G Hayes. 15 – schaef71, Dean Bouton, Sheri Lim. 16 – logika600. 17 – Marten_House, Damsea. 18 – BMJ, Wendy Rentz. 19 – Carrie Olson, Donna A. Herrmann. 20 – John Carnemolla, Kletr. 21 – Alta Oosthuizen, Vishnevskiy Vasily. 22 – LouieLea, Menno Schaefer. 23 – PJ photography, Rudmer Zwerver. 24 – Sergey 402. 25 – sirtravelalot, Joey_Danuphol, Roger Clark ARPS. 26 – Vasik Olga, Mr.anaked. 27 – Tory Kallman, Dmytro Zinkevych, lev radin. 28 – Camptoloma, Adwo, Bernd Wolter. 29 – sompreaw, EcoPrint, Collins93. 30 – Belle Ciezak, axily.

# CONTENTS

PAGE 4   What Is Reproduction?
PAGE 6   Different Types of Bird
PAGE 8   Courtship
PAGE 10  Mating
PAGE 12  Nesting
PAGE 16  Bird Eggs
PAGE 18  Bird Young
PAGE 20  Bird Parents
PAGE 22  Reproduction in Puffins
PAGE 24  Reproduction in Emperor Penguins
PAGE 26  Birds Under Threat
PAGE 28  Fascinating Facts
PAGE 31  Glossary
PAGE 32  Index

Words that look like THIS can be found in the glossary on page 31.

# WHAT IS REPRODUCTION?

Have you ever wondered how you and all the other animals and plants in our world came to be here? Where did we all come from? These are big questions, but the answer is simple – reproduction. Reproduction is the process by which all living things make more of themselves. It is common to all living things, from the blue whale, the largest animal on Earth, to the tiniest living things that can only be seen under a microscope. Mammals, birds, fish, reptiles, amphibians, insects and plants all need to reproduce. You are here because your parents have reproduced, as their parents did before them.

These grandparents and parents have reproduced to give birth to new GENERATIONS.

## WHY IS REPRODUCTION IMPORTANT?

Reproduction is important because all living things have a LIFESPAN and will eventually die. They must therefore reproduce to make sure that their SPECIES continues and does not die out. This is sometimes called 'the circle of life'.

THE EARLIEST RELATIVES OF BIRDS WERE SMALL, MEAT-EATING DINOSAURS CALLED THEROPODS.

Blue flycatchers protecting their BROOD of chicks in the nest

# SEXUAL AND ASEXUAL REPRODUCTION

Sexual reproduction requires one male and one female parent. New life is made by putting together genetic information (instructions about how growth and development take place) from the two parents. Genetic information is found inside CELLS, including sex cells called gametes. In males, gametes are called sperm. In females, gametes are called eggs. During sexual reproduction, the two gametes join together in a process called fertilisation. When an egg cell and a sperm cell join together, they form a fertilised egg. This then begins to divide over and over again to form an EMBRYO. The embryo grows to become a new lifeform that carries similar genetic information to both parents but is not exactly the same as either.

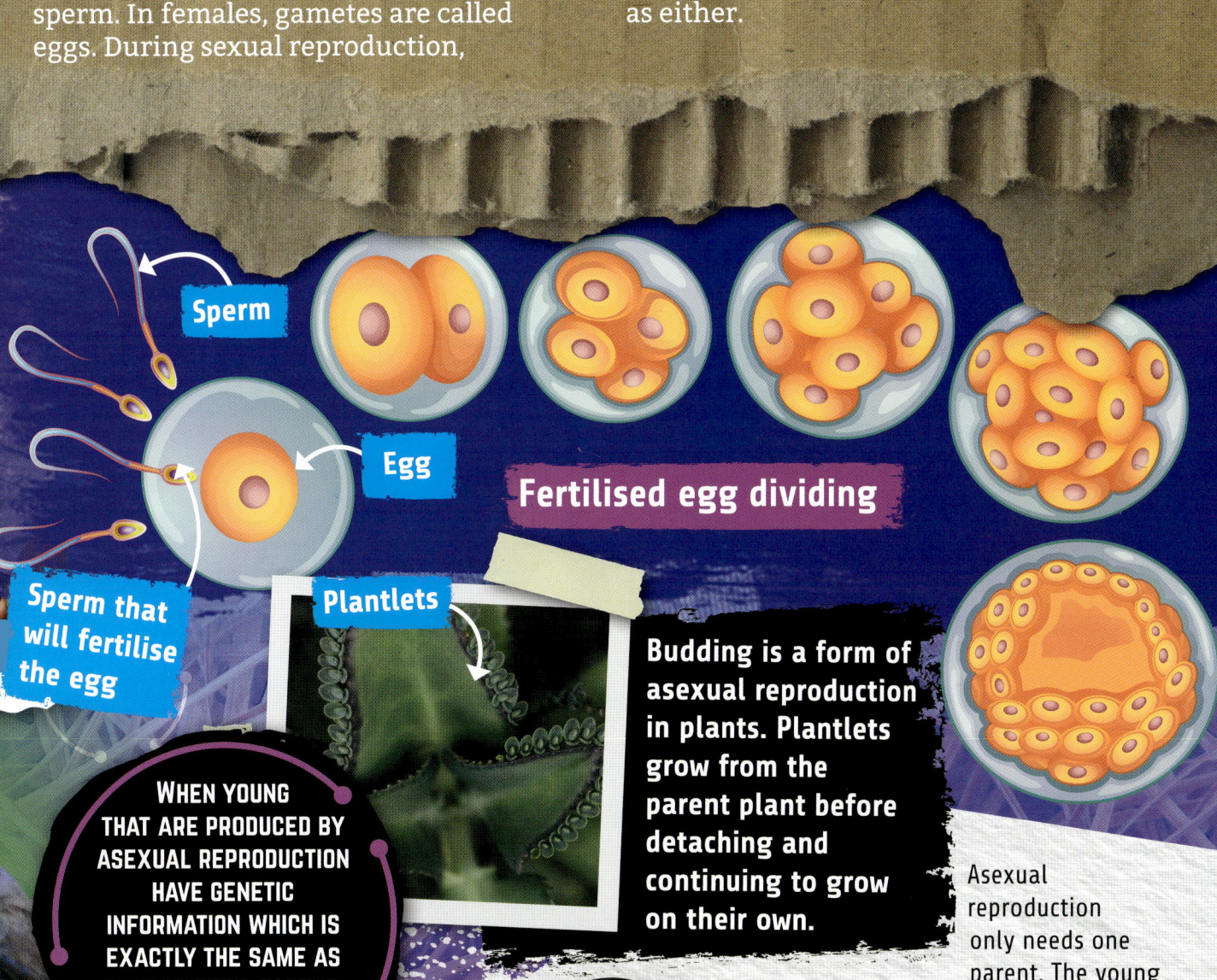

Budding is a form of asexual reproduction in plants. Plantlets grow from the parent plant before detaching and continuing to grow on their own.

WHEN YOUNG THAT ARE PRODUCED BY ASEXUAL REPRODUCTION HAVE GENETIC INFORMATION WHICH IS EXACTLY THE SAME AS THAT OF THEIR PARENT, THEY ARE CALLED CLONES.

Asexual reproduction only needs one parent. The young that are produced carry exactly the same genetic information as the parent. Asexual reproduction may take place as a result of a process called parthenogenesis (say: par-thu-no-jen-u-sis), in which eggs develop into embryos without having been fertilised by sperm. Budding, FRAGMENTATION and FISSION are other common forms of asexual reproduction. Asexual reproduction is very rare in animals but is commonly seen in BACTERIA, fungi and plants.

*Sexual reproduction for us then, as we're not plants, bacteria or fungi.*

*But you are a fun guy – you always make me laugh!*

# DIFFERENT TYPES OF BIRD

The animal kingdom is divided into smaller groups called phyla. Phyla group together animals that are alike in important ways. Along with mammals, fish, reptiles and amphibians, birds are vertebrates. This means that they have a backbone. Unlike most vertebrates, however, birds have a skeleton filled with hollows and air pockets. These make their skeletons light and help them to fly. Phyla are divided into smaller groups called classes. Birds belong to a class called Aves. Like mammals, birds are warm-blooded. This means that they can keep their body temperature the same, whatever the temperature of their environment.

In cold weather, birds can fluff up their feathers to trap body heat and keep themselves warm.

Scientists think that there are around 10,000 different bird species.

## BIRD CHECKLIST
- Have waterproof skin
- Are covered in feathers that help them to fly, keep them warm and may help to CAMOUFLAGE them
- Lay hard-shelled, waterproof eggs
- Have a beak or bill rather than teeth
- Have two legs ADAPTED for perching as well as walking
- Have two wings
- Most are able to fly

Ostriches are unusual birds. They cannot fly, but can run at speeds up to 70 kilometres per hour (kph).

Birds are found on every continent of the world, on land and in freshwater and saltwater HABITATS. They live in every type of habitat including mountains, deserts, tropical rainforests and freezing ice sheets. Some escape from cold weather by MIGRATING to warmer countries.

# BIRD ORDER

The class to which birds belong is broken down into around 28 smaller groups called orders. Here are some examples:

FALCONIFORMES (RAPTORS)
– Meat-eating hunters
– Include eagles, falcons, hawks, vultures and osprey
– Often have sharp TALONS to catch PREY

This bald eagle is using its talons to catch fish.

PASSERIFORMES (SONGBIRDS)
– Make up almost half of all bird species
– Include magpies, starlings, nightingales and larks
– Have three toes that point forwards and one that faces back, allowing them to perch safely on branches, grasses and bird feeders

The tuneful song of the nightingale is considered one of the most beautiful bird songs.

STRIGIFORMES (OWLS)
– Able to fly almost silently
– Able to turn their heads far enough to see behind their bodies
– Have excellent hearing and the best night vision in the animal kingdom

Snowy owls are perfectly camouflaged to suit their snowy habitats.

7

# COURTSHIP

Birds use lots of different courting behaviours to attract a partner and to show that they are ready to mate. These behaviours show off their strength, health, intelligence and ability to reproduce. They help the female to choose the partner most likely to produce healthy young. Courtship behaviours also help to make sure that birds of the same species mate with one another.

## DISPLAYS

Some male birds use displays of brightly coloured feathers to show off their health and strength. Those with long tails, such as pheasants and peafowl, lift up their train of feathers and fan it out. Some birds attract attention using head feathers called a crest. Others show off their markings, <u>IRIDESCENT</u> feathers or brightly coloured beaks.

The male frigate bird attracts the attention of a mate by puffing up the red pouch on his chest.

The male red-capped manakin chooses a branch with no leaves so the female can see his fancy footwork clearly.

## DANCING

Courtship dancing includes wing-flapping, head-bobbing, diving, bill-rubbing and special steps. Mistakes in the movements show weakness and do not impress the females who are watching. In some species, the male and female dance together, but usually the male dances while the female watches.

8

## SINGING

Singing is one of the most common courtship behaviours. The male tries to impress the female by singing many different songs. His singing skills show off his intelligence and skill, which are things that the female is looking for in her mate. Usually only the male sings in courtship, but in some species the male and female sing together. Birds also use singing to mark out their particular area (their territory) and to warn off other males from their nesting site.

## FEEDING

The male brings food to the female to prove that he can find and share food. In some species, the male puts food, such as an insect or seed, directly into the female's mouth. This shows her that he will be able to help feed her chicks once they have hatched in the nest.

The female is likely to choose a mate who is able to find food for her and her chicks.

Gannets in a nesting COLONY PREENING one another

## PREENING

Male and female birds may preen each other, lean against one another or sit very close together. These behaviours strengthen the bond between them and show that they will not try to hurt one another.

# MATING

Birds reproduce sexually. All birds have a single opening through which they get rid of urine and faeces (wee and poo). This opening is called the cloaca. It may also be called the vent. Female birds, and most male birds, use the cloaca for reproduction. When a bird is ready to mate, the cloaca swells so that is sticks out slightly from the rest of the body. A male bird climbs onto the female's back to mate. The male and female mate by positioning themselves so that their cloacas touch. This is sometimes called a cloacal kiss. It only takes a few seconds. Sperm from the male passes to the female through her cloaca. It then travels into the female's body where fertilisation takes place. The fertilised egg then goes through several stages until it is ready to be laid. In a few species, including ducks, geese, swans, ostriches and emus, the male has an ORGAN called a penis. This is used to insert sperm directly inside the female's body.

**Cloaca**

A bird's cloaca is found underneath the base of the tail. During mating, the female moves her tail to one side.

**MOST BIRDS MATE FOR ONLY ONE BREEDING SEASON, BUT SOME, SUCH AS EAGLES AND SWANS, MATE FOR LIFE. OTHERS, SUCH AS HUMMINGBIRDS, HAVE MANY MATES IN THE SAME SEASON.**

Blue-tailed bee-eaters mating

Do blue-tailed bee-eaters really eat bees?

Yes, and wasps.

Yuck!

# THE BREEDING SEASON

Spring is the breeding season for most birds. As the days get longer and the temperature starts to warm up, birds are able to tell that spring has arrived. They time their breeding season so that there will be plenty of food available when the chicks hatch. In desert areas, sudden rains can trigger mating. In these habitats, plants have EVOLVED that bloom quickly when it rains. These plants provide food for nesting birds and their chicks. Some species have a long INCUBATION PERIOD, produce several broods of eggs each season or give their chicks several weeks of care after hatching. For these species, the breeding season begins earlier, so that there is enough time for the young to be cared for properly. Birds that build a new nest every year usually breed later than those that reuse an old nest. This is because they need time to collect their nesting materials, such as twigs and grasses.

Swallows and other birds that migrate during the winter start looking for nesting sites as soon as they return in the spring.

Crossbills time their breeding so that there are plenty of pine cone seeds available to feed their young, even if that means starting to breed in the winter months.

# NESTING

House martins nesting

Most birds build a nest of some sort. It must provide a safe place for the eggs to be incubated and for the chicks to live until they are ready to leave. Some birds, such as swifts, may return to the same nest year after year. Others build a new nest each year. Most nests are only used once. Even species that raise several broods of young each breeding season, such as blackbirds, usually build a new nest each time. They often reuse materials from the first nest. Some birds build big, complicated nests, while others simply scrape a hole in the ground. Some build their nests in trees or bushes, while others choose the roofs or gutters of buildings.

Orioles build cosy bag-like nests. They are lined with feathers or animal wool and hang from tree branches.

THE MALE HOUSE WREN BUILDS UP TO 12 NESTS TO TRY TO IMPRESS THE FEMALE, WHO THEN CHOOSES WHICH ONE SHE WANTS TO CALL HOME.

Some birds, such as thrushes, weave cup-shaped nests made of twigs, grasses and reeds. These may be lined with mud and camouflaged with moss. Tiny hummingbirds build nests made of materials such as spider webs and soft plant materials. These stretchy nests can grow as the young chicks get bigger.

Edible-nest swiftlets have an extraordinary way of making their nests, high on the roofs and walls of caves. During the breeding season, the male dribbles long, gooey strands of saliva (spit). He then uses his beak to weave them into a basket-shaped nest. The strands slowly harden so that the nest is firm and safe. Swiftlets nest in huge colonies made up of thousands of birds. Soup made from the nests is thought of as an expensive treat in some Asian countries and so the nests are often taken by POACHERS.

The nests are built up in layers.

Woodpeckers make a rhythmic drumming sound as they peck a tree to make a nesting site. The noise attracts mates and warns off other males.

Holes in trees, riverbanks or walls make safe nesting sites for some birds. Some reuse a hole made by another animal. Those that have strong bills, such as the woodpecker, make their own.

Some habitats, such as grasslands, have few trees or other safe nesting sites. Birds in these habitats may lay their eggs on the ground or even under it. Some burrowing owls, for example, dig out a burrow, while others use burrows that have been abandoned by digging animals such as badgers or armadillos.

Burrowing owl

Some large birds, including eagles, ospreys and storks, build huge nests that they return to each spring. The nests are made of sticks and small branches, and lined with softer materials, such as grasses. Each year, the male and female add to the nest, making it larger and safer. These birds usually nest in tall, sturdy trees or other places high above the ground.

The nest of this family of storks has been built on a chimney.

Cactus wren building its nest

There are few places for birds to build nests in the desert, but the cactus wren has found a clever solution to the problem. It builds its nest among the branches of thorny desert cacti. The sharp spines of the cacti do not seem to harm the cactus wren, but they protect the nest from PREDATORS such as snakes. The nest is the size and shape of a football and is entered through a tunnel-like passage. Cactus wrens have up to three broods of chicks each year and the hardworking male builds nests all year round for his growing family.

Whoa! That looks like a scary place to nest.

I can't watch!

Don't panic! Let's look at page 24 to find out what we do.

Some water birds, such as ducks, build their nests away from the water. Others, such as grebes, build nests that float on the surface. They dive down to the bottom of the lake or stream and bring rotting plant material and mud back to the surface. They slowly pile everything up to make a nesting platform. Even after the eggs have been laid, they continue to add more materials to keep the nest afloat. The plant material gives off heat as it rots. This helps the eggs to hatch.

The grebe fixes its nest to tall reeds or other plants, which hide the nest from predators.

Some birds, such as guillemots, nest in huge colonies on rocky sea cliffs. Rather than building a nest, they lay their eggs on narrow ledges where the eggs are safe from predators. Condors and falcons may use inland cliffs, building nests made of sticks in the rocky CREVICES. Beach-nesting birds, such as terns and plovers, lay their eggs in shallow dips scraped out of the sand. These eggs are usually well camouflaged, with speckles matching the pebbles or grains of sand.

These plover eggs are well camouflaged. Can you spot four eggs?

A nesting colony of guillemots

15

# BIRD EGGS

Eggshell
Shell membranes
Albumen
Chalazae
Yolk
Air sac

A bird's eggs are formed in an organ called the ovary, where a yolk is added. The yolk will be the food store for the developing embryo. The egg then passes into a tube called the oviduct, where it is fertilised by sperm from the male. Membranes and albumen (egg white) are then added. Membranes are thin layers that protect the contents (insides) of the egg. Albumen is the liquid in which the growing embryo will develop. As the egg passes along the oviduct, it turns. This produces twisted strands called chalazae. These are attached to the yolk sac and hold the yolk in place in the centre of the egg. The shell is added last, just before the egg is laid. Colours and markings are added by special cells in the oviduct walls.

**AS WELL AS CAMOUFLAGING AN EGG, A COLOURED SHELL IS ALSO THOUGHT TO ACT LIKE SUNSCREEN, PROTECTING THE EMBRYO FROM HARMFUL SUNRAYS.**

All birds are oviparous. This means that they lay eggs that hatch outside the body. After the eggs have been laid, a parent incubates them until they hatch, which means keeping them warm by sitting on the nest.

## CLUTCH SIZE

The total number of eggs laid at each nesting is called the clutch size. Different species have different clutch sizes. The albatross normally lays only one egg, but emus can lay up to 15. A single chick hatches from each egg.

**Seabirds like this kittiwake usually lay only one or two eggs.**

The hummingbird lays two white eggs that look like small jellybeans.

## SHAPE AND SIZE

When we say that something is egg-shaped, we mean that it has the shape of an egg that we might eat. In fact, different species lay eggs with all sorts of shapes. Owls lay round eggs like golf balls, while fast-flying birds such as swallows and swifts usually lay long, oval-shaped eggs. Birds that lay their eggs on cliff ledges lay pointy eggs. If the eggs are bumped, they spin round in a circle, rather than rolling off the cliff edge. The largest eggs are laid by the ostrich. These may weigh up to 1.2 kilograms. The smallest are laid by the hummingbird.

I wonder what my eggs will look like. Let's read on and find out.

17

# BIRD YOUNG

Eggshells have thousands of tiny holes called pores. The OXYGEN that the embryo needs to survive passes through these pores. Shortly before hatching, the chick breaks into the air sac. This forms inside the egg when it is laid and gets larger as the embryo develops. The chick now begins to use its lungs to breathe oxygen from the air sac. At this stage, the chick may make a 'peeping' sound.

**Herring gull eggs beginning to hatch**

## BREAKING FREE

Before hatching, a chick grows a small, sharp lump called a caruncle on its beak. The caruncle is often called an egg tooth. The chick uses its egg tooth to crack the shell. It also uses its legs and shoulders to press against the shell. The chick then moves round in a circle inside the egg, chipping away at the inside of the shell. This is called pipping and is very tiring for the young chick. In the end, the top of the shell falls away and the chick breaks free.

The first of four robins has just hatched.

ADULT BIRDS MAKE FLYING LOOK EASY, BUT CHICKS HAVE TO LEARN TO FLY. SOME PARENTS PUSH THE CHICKS OUT OF THE NEST, ESPECIALLY WHEN THEIR LOUD CALLS ARE ATTRACTING PREDATORS.

# PRECOCIAL AND ALTRICIAL YOUNG

The chicks of some species are born well developed, with fluffy feathers and their eyes open. They can stand and walk about on their own. These chicks are described as precocial (say: pre-co-shul). Precocial species include ducks, chickens and turkeys. Some precocial chicks can even feed themselves soon after hatching.

**Ducklings may leave the nest with their mother just one day after hatching.**

Altricial (say: al-trish-ul) species have young that are helpless when they hatch. They have no feathers or only a light covering, called down. Their eyes are closed, and they cannot hold their heads up. The parents have to carry on incubating the chicks to keep them warm as they cannot control their body temperature, even for a short time. The chicks also have to be fed in the nest. These kinds of species include songbirds, pigeons and kingfishers.

**Newly hatched house finch chicks call to their parents for food straightaway.**

Down

# FLEDGING

Most songbirds are ready to fledge (leave the nest) after two to three weeks. Other species, such as hawks, eagles and owls, may stay in the nest for seven to ten weeks. Once they leave, chicks may stay close to their parents while they learn to survive on their own.

19

# BIRD PARENTS

Birds usually start to incubate their eggs once they have all been laid so that they all hatch at about the same time. Some, such as herons and cormorants, begin incubation as soon as the first egg is laid. Different species have different incubation periods. Generally, the larger the bird, the longer the incubation period. In some species, such as blackbirds and robins, only the mother incubates the eggs. In others, such as house sparrows, both parents take it in turns. In a few species, such as dotterels, only the male incubates the eggs and raises the chicks.

Royal albatross parents with their chick

The eggs of small songbirds usually hatch in about 11 days, but those of the royal albatross take up to 80 days.

Both blue tit parents feed the chicks. It's hard work as each chick can eat 100 caterpillars a day.

SPOTTED SANDPIPER FATHERS DO ALMOST ALL OF THE INCUBATING AND CARING FOR THE CHICKS.

## FEEDING

Some birds carry food such as caterpillars and insects back to the nest for the young. Others, such as crows, swallow food and then REGURGITATE it for the chicks later. Some birds, such as wood pigeons, make a special liquid called crop milk, which they regurgitate for their young. Raptors (birds of prey) carry their prey back to the nest, where they tear it into small chunks for the chicks.

The belly feathers of the namaqua sandgrouse are adapted for soaking up and holding water.

## DOTING DADS

In most animal species, care of the young by the male is rare, but among birds, it is common. Males are often the nest builders. They also often share defending the nesting site and incubating and feeding the young with the female. Namaqua sandgrouse males are excellent fathers. These birds nest in hot, dry areas and the male flies many kilometres to find water for the chicks. He then soaks his feathers before returning to give his family a drink.

This marsh warbler is feeding a common cuckoo chick that has hatched in its nest.

## BROOD PARASITES

Some birds, known as brood parasites, do not bother to make a nest or care for their young at all. They simply lay their egg in a nest built by another species. They then abandon the egg, leaving it to the care of the other parents. These parents care for the egg and chick as if it were their own. The cuckoo is the best-known example of a brood parasite. Cuckoo chicks usually hatch first and may roll the eggs of the host species out of the nest or throw the other chicks out after they hatch.

*It's not easy looking after chicks, is it?*

*No, but we've got to do our bit to keep our species going.*

21

# REPRODUCTION IN PUFFINS

Puffins live in the open waters of the Atlantic Ocean. They reach sexual maturity (the age at which they are ready to reproduce) at around five years old. During the breeding and nesting seasons, they are found on rocky coastlines, in huge colonies of thousands of birds. The adult birds return to their colonies in spring. At first, they form large groups called rafts, just off the coast, before coming ashore to breed. Puffins usually mate for life and return to the same nest site each year.

Puffins choose rocky coastlines for breeding.

**Puffins can live for more than 20 years.**

## PUFFIN COUPLES

Puffins' beaks are normally grey but, in the mating season, they turn bright orange. It is thought that this helps the birds to find their mates again. Some couples perform courtship behaviour called billing, in which they rub their beaks together. Males who have not yet found a mate may fight with other males for a female or a suitable nesting site. They puff up their feathers to make themselves look bigger, open their wings and beaks, stamp their feet and wrestle with one another.

Male and female puffins billing

# NESTING

Puffins are burrowing birds. They may dig a burrow into the soil at the tops of cliffs or use an old rabbit burrow. Both parents then build a nest with grasses, feathers and seaweed inside the burrow. If there is nowhere to burrow, puffins may nest under boulders or in crevices in the cliffs. The female lays only one egg. Both parents take it in turns to incubate the egg, which hatches after about 40 days.

Puffins burrow into the soil with their beaks and shovel dirt out behind them using their feet.

# FEEDING AND FLEDGING

Both parents take turns fishing for food for the chick, called a puffling. Puffins have specially adapted beaks that help them to hold prey firmly and to dive for more, even if they already have fish in their mouths. The puffling stays inside the burrow until its flight feathers have developed and it is able to fly. This takes between 34 and 60 days. The parents leave the puffling shortly before it is ready to leave the nest. The puffling then heads for the sea, where it lives before coming ashore to breed.

Pufflings normally head for the sea when it is dark, using the moon and stars to guide them. Human sources of light, like street lamps, sometimes confuse them so that they head the wrong way.

This puffin has a mouthful of eels for its hungry chick.

23

# REPRODUCTION IN EMPEROR PENGUINS

Emperor penguins are the largest of the 18 species of penguin. They spend their lives in the cold waters of the Antarctic and breed on sea ice or inland ice shelves, forming large colonies. The breeding season begins in autumn, when the sea ice becomes thick enough to support the weight of the colony. Penguins have only one mate each breeding season and some mate for life.

**There may be thousands of birds in a breeding colony.**

## PENGUIN COUPLES

Male emperor penguins attract a female and warn off other males by bowing and swinging their heads. They also squawk or 'bray'. Once they have paired off, the male and female walk through the colony. The male walks behind the female. Before mating, they bow to one another. After mating, the female lays one egg. There are no nesting materials in the Antarctic, but the egg must be kept warm and off the ice. The female carefully passes the egg to the male. He then balances it on his feet and covers it with a special skin fold called a brood pouch.

**Because the Antarctic is in the Southern Hemisphere, autumn starts in March.**

## INCUBATION

While the male incubates the egg, the female heads off to sea to feed. It takes up to 75 days for the eggs to hatch. During this time, males have no food. They use their stored body fat to survive and they huddle together for warmth. From time to time, those on the outside of the huddle are moved into the middle to warm up. Newly hatched chicks weigh only about 200 grams and have only a thin layer of down. The female returns in mid-winter and the parents work together to keep the chick safe, warm and fed.

> The outside temperature may drop as low as -60 degrees Celsius (°C), but the brood pouch keeps the egg warm at around 38°C.

> Without the protection of the brood pouch, a newly hatched chick could die in a few minutes.

> Emperor penguins reach sexual maturity at around three years old, but often wait another two years before returning to their colony to breed for the first time.

## GROWING UP

By the start of spring, the chicks have grown a thick covering of down and are growing quickly. The colony is noisy and full of activity as the parents come and go with fish for their young. Chicks that are left alone while both parents are collecting food huddle for warmth. By mid-summer, the chicks have grown adult feathers. Soon after, the parents leave and the chicks find their own way to sea.

> Growing takes a lot of energy and the chicks are always hungry.

*I hope we don't drop the egg.*

25

# BIRDS UNDER THREAT

Birds play a very important part in the world's ECOSYSTEMS, as both predators and prey in the FOOD CHAIN. Unfortunately, they face serious threats, mostly due to human activities. It is thought that one in eight bird species is now threatened with EXTINCTION worldwide. Even species that were once very common, such as turtle doves and snowy owls, are now classed as being under threat of extinction.

The yellow-breasted bunting is CRITICALLY ENDANGERED.

Birds can die after being caught in plastic waste, and swallowing plastic can stop them from feeding and reproducing.

## WHAT THREATS ARE BIRDS FACING?

Threats faced by birds include hunting and loss of habitat. Hunting may remove young birds that have not yet reproduced or parents caring for chicks. The grey parrot, for example, is now classed as endangered in the wild, partly due to illegal hunting. DEFORESTATION of its natural habitat across central Africa is also to blame. Overfishing is a serious threat for seabirds such as kittiwakes and puffins that catch fish to feed their young. Plastic pollution of oceans and coastal areas is also a big problem. Around 8 million tons of plastic ends up in our oceans every year.

Bird reproduction is also threatened by oil spills at sea and by products used in farming being washed into rivers and oceans. GLOBAL WARMING is also a serious problem. Rising sea temperatures mean there are lower levels of PLANKTON, which are eaten by fish. In turn, this means less food for seabirds and their young. Global warming will also raise sea levels, resulting in a loss of bird habitats such as mudflats and marshes. The breeding grounds of shore-nesting birds, such as terns, are likely to be flooded.

Worldwide, three-quarters of breeding Laysan albatrosses are found on Midway Atoll, a low-lying part of Hawaii. Rising seas could flood their nesting grounds.

Television programmes made by conservationists such as Sir David Attenborough have helped to teach people about endangered birds.

## HOW YOU CAN HELP

You can help to reduce plastic pollution by reusing and recycling plastic materials. Global warming is caused by the burning of FOSSIL FUELS for transport, heating and to make electricity. Think about how you and your family can use less electricity. Turn off lights, televisions and computers that are not being used. Maybe you could walk to school instead of taking the car. Try to get involved with charities such as the World Wide Fund for Nature (WWF) that support bird conservation projects.

THE WWF IS A CONSERVATION CHARITY. IT IS WORKING TO STOP THE ILLEGAL PET TRADE IN BRIGHTLY COLOURED MACAW PARROTS FROM THE AMAZON RAINFOREST.

27

# FASCINATING FACTS

As we have seen, the young of some species have special names. Young swans, for example, are called cygnets and young doves are called squabs. What others can you think of?

A mute swan with her cygnets

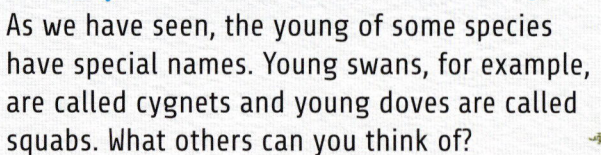

The blue-footed booby bird looks like it has stepped in a can of blue paint. The male shows off his feet in a courtship dance, stamping and high-stepping to impress the female. The bluer his feet, the more likely she is to be impressed and mate with him.

During the mating season, male and female great crested grebes develop black and orange ruffs and black ear tufts, known as tippets. Courtship displays include flicking their heads from side to side to show off the ruffs and tippets. Finally, they dive down and return with weed in their bills. They then meet, chest to chest, and paddle furiously to raise themselves high up out of the water.

The courtship 'weed dance' of the grebe

Birds use any materials they can find to build their nests. In towns and cities, they may pick up sweet wrappers or other small pieces of rubbish. The Australian yellow-faced honeyeater even steals fur from the backs of koalas to line its nest.

Sociable weaver birds work together to build one huge nest that may be up to eight metres across. Inside, there may be up to 100 separate nesting sections.

**Yellow-faced honeyeater**

**The nest is like an apartment block for birds.**

**The peregrine falcon can dive at speeds of up to 300 kph and catch prey in the air.**

Red-breasted geese would usually be prey for peregrine falcons. The geese only breed in northern Russia and, during the breeding season, sometimes nest just a few metres from falcon nests. The falcons protect the young in their own nests from snowy owls and Arctic foxes by diving and screeching. This behaviour also protects the geese nests. In return, the loud alarm calls of the geese act as an early warning system for the falcons that predators are nearby.

The Australian brush-turkey uses rotting plant material to cover its eggs. The rotting process gives off the heat that is needed for the eggs to hatch. The brush-turkey cleverly keeps the eggs at just the right temperature by adding more vegetation if the eggs are too cold or removing some if the eggs are too hot.

**The brush-turkey uses its huge feet to gather the rotting vegetation.**

An aquarium in Sydney, Australia, is home to two male gentoo penguins named Sphen and Magic – or Sphengic. These two penguins became a couple and began gathering pebbles to build a nest. As two males, they could not produce an egg of their own. Fortunately, gentoo penguins often lay two eggs, so a second egg from another couple was given to Sphengic. The pair proved to be excellent parents. They incubated the egg successfully and, when the chick hatched, they carried on working together to care for it. Although it is rare for two male penguins to raise a chick, it is quite common for males to court one another in the breeding season.

**In the wild, gentoo penguins like these are under threat from plastic pollution and global warming.**

# GLOSSARY

**ADAPTED** changed over time to suit different conditions

**BACTERIA** tiny, single-celled organisms

**BROOD** a family of chicks or other young animals produced at one hatching

**CAMOUFLAGE** a way of hiding something so it looks like its surroundings

**CELLS** the basic units that make up all living things

**COLONY** a large group of birds that nest in a particular area

**CREVICES** narrow gaps in rock

**CRITICALLY ENDANGERED** threatened to the point of becoming almost extinct

**DEFORESTATION** the cutting down and removal of trees in a forest

**ECOSYSTEMS** groups of all the living things such as animals and non-living things such as soil that exist in a particular place and rely on one another for survival

**EMBRYO** an unborn or unhatched young in the process of development

**EVOLVED** changed gradually into different forms

**EXTINCTION** the process by which a species dies out completely

**FISSION** a form of asexual reproduction in which the parent cells of an organism divide to make new cells that are exactly the same as the parent cells

**FOOD CHAIN** a series of organisms in which each depends on the next as a source of food

**FOSSIL FUELS** fuels, such as coal, oil and gas, that formed millions of years ago from the remains of animals and plants

**FRAGMENTATION** a form of asexual reproduction in which the organism splits into fragments, each of which becomes a new individual that is exactly the same as the parent

**GENERATIONS** groups of animals of the same species that are roughly the same age

**GLOBAL WARMING** the gradual rise in the Earth's temperature

**HABITATS** the natural environments in which animals or plants live

**INCUBATION PERIOD** the time between eggs being laid and hatching, during which they must be kept warm

**IRIDESCENT** showing different colours that seem to change when looked at from different angles, as in the case of a soap bubble

**LIFESPAN** the period of time for which a person, animal or plant lives or is expected to live

**MIGRATING** moving from one habitat or region to another when the seasons change

**ORGAN** a part of the body, such as the heart or liver, that has a particular function

**OXYGEN** a colourless gas found in air that is essential for life

**PLANKTON** tiny living creatures that float and drift in seas and rivers and play an important part in the food chain

**POACHERS** people who capture animals illegally

**PREDATORS** animals that hunt other animals for food

**PREENING** to tidy and clean the feathers

**PREY** animals that are hunted by other animals for food

**REGURGITATE** bring swallowed food up again into the mouth

**SPECIES** a group of very similar animals or plants that can produce young together

**TALONS** the claws of an animal, especially a bird of prey

# INDEX

**A**
air sacs 16, 18
albumen 16
Attenborough, Sir David 27

**B**
beaks 6, 8, 13, 18, 22–23
bills 6, 8, 13, 28
breeding season 10–13, 24, 29–30
brood parasites 21
brood pouches 24–25
burrows 13, 23

**C**
camouflage 6–7, 12, 15–16
cells 5, 16
chalazae 16
chicks
 – altricial 19
 – precocial 19
cloacal kisses 10
cloacas 10
clutches 16
conservation 27
courtship 8–9, 22, 28, 30

**D**
down 19, 25

**E**
ecosystems 26
egg teeth 18
eggs 5–6, 10–13, 15–18, 20–21, 23–25, 30
embryos 5, 16, 18
evolution 11
extinction 26

**F**
feathers 6, 8, 12, 19, 21–23, 25
fertilisation 5, 10, 16
fledging 19, 23
food chains 26
fossil fuels 27

**G**
gametes 5
global warming 27, 30

**H**
habitats 7, 11, 13, 26–27

**I**
incubation 11–12, 16, 19–21, 23, 25, 30

**M**
mating 8, 10–11, 22, 24, 28
membranes 16
migration 7, 11

**N**
nesting materials 11–12, 14–15, 24, 29–30
nests 4, 9, 11–16, 18–21, 23, 29–30

**O**
ovaries 16
oviducts 16
oviparity 16

**P**
parthenogenesis 5
pipping 18
predators 14–15, 18, 26, 29
prey 7, 20, 23, 26, 29
pollution 26–27, 30

**R**
reproduction
 – asexual 5
 – sexual 5

**S**
sexual maturity (age of) 22, 25
shells 6, 16, 18
sperm 5, 10, 16

**T**
tails 8, 10
talons 7

**W**
wings 6, 8, 22
WWF (World Wide Fund for Nature) 27

**Y**
yolks 16